RAISING
KING

Poems by Joseph Ross

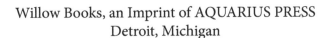

Willow Books, an Imprint of AQUARIUS PRESS
Detroit, Michigan

RAISING KING: poems

Editor: Randall Horton
Cover photo: Marion S. Trikoso
Cover design: Jonathan Moises Olivares

Reprinted by arrangement with The Heirs to the Estate of Martin Luther King, Jr., c/o Writers House as agent for the proprietor, New York, NY.

ISBN 978-1-7348273-8-5
LCCN 2020944088

Acknowledgments
All page numbers in *Stride Toward Freedom* come from the King Legacy edition, published by Beacon Press. Page numbers in *Why We Can't Wait* come from the Signet Classics edition, published by Penguin Books. Page numbers in *Where Do We Go from Here: Chaos or Community?* come from the King Legacy edition, published by Beacon Press.

Thanks to the editors of the following journals who published these poems, sometimes in slightly different forms:

"1963" *Southern Quarterly*
"Midnight" *Seminary Ridge Journal*
"A Waning Crescent" *The Night's Magician: Poems about the Moon*
"My Brother's Keeper" *Poet Lore*

Willow Books, an Imprint of Aquarius Press
www.WillowLit.net

Aquarius Press LLC
PO Box 23096
Detroit, MI 48223
www.AquariusPress.net

Contents

Dedication

to Orlando Pinder, whose artistic talent, passion, and kindness
build Dr. King's Beloved Community every day

to Katie Murphy, my teaching colleague,
who helps her students imagine Dr. King's dream

to Robert, always, with love.

Introduction

Reverend Martin Luther King, Jr. lived a prophetic and compassionate life. Like the prophets of the Old Testament, he stared directly at injustice, named it plainly, then worked to change it. His writings and nonviolent protests find their source in the actions of prophets like Jeremiah. His strong hope mirrors the prophet Isaiah. At the root of his writing and activism lives a deep well of compassion. He knew the indignities suffered by African Americans as he felt them in his own skin. Further, he knew racism disfigured the white people who used it. Thus, he focused his life in such a way, built on compassion, that his work might free both those who suffer from racism and those who inflict the suffering. Dr. King also understood the massive damage of militarism and materialism. He saw American culture infected with these enormous challenges and thus tried to communicate the danger and heal it at the same time.

His prophetic and compassionate life, I am convinced, can help build a more peaceful and just world, if more people studied it and imitated it. I have believed this for many years. How might this be? How might our world be more peaceful and just if more people understood his life and work? Imagine an America whose political and spiritual leaders help build a "person-centered" society rather than a "thing-centered" society. Imagine an America in which individuals seek to heal differences rather than defeat others? Imagine a world where adults teach children to avoid the damage that racism does both to the oppressed and the oppressors? Imagine a world where we understand that militarism destroys everything and does not protect anything.

I began teaching Dr. King's life in a Freshman Seminar course at the University of Notre Dame in 1988. I later taught a composition course on his life at American University in Washington, D.C. While many people know his "I Have a Dream" speech, his "Beloved Community" and "World House" are not understood. These ideas challenge us, they call for deeper transformation.

Three of Dr. King's books are sometimes called his political autobiographies. *Stride Toward Freedom* (1958) shows us Dr. King in his late twenties. This book recalls the Montgomery, Alabama bus protest. *Why We Can't Wait* (1963) explores the violent events of 1963 and includes his "Letter from Birmingham Jail." He is more aware of the cost of nonviolence. *Where Do We Go from Here?* (1968) written in the final year of his life, reveals an urgent man hoping to heal our interconnected but wounded world.

This collection of poems uses these three books to explore Dr. King's life in poems. The poems speak in varied voices: sometimes Dr. King's voice, sometimes a voice connected to a specific event, sometimes my own. Each poem carries an epigraph of Dr. King's words about a specific event or idea. Each section closes with a poem in the voice of Coretta Scott King, whose sacrifices made Dr. King's work possible. I hope these poems honor Dr. King by remembering his vision and his deep love for our often-broken world.

Joseph Ross

Martin Luther King, Jr.—Prologue

1

In the beginning
was a boat, swollen

with humans, history
would call slaves.

The men who loved
these boats thought

they knew Jesus.
They prayed Jesus,

they ate Jesus. Their
boat cut the waters

like a whip, leaving
a weeping scent

in its churning wake.
The moon lit

the water around
the boat, but the moon

did not light the boat.
The boat worked

through the waters
in the dark.

Now the boat is dust.
The whip

survives.

2

A man came
who was not a slave.

He was not the moon,
its light, or the water.

Like the boats before him,
he too cut the water.

But he was not
the whip. He had

bones the whip
could not reach.

But he was not
the bones. He had

light to cut
the darkness. But he

was not the light. He
met the darkness

when the whip became
a bullet.

The man stood
and the bullet came.

His bones are dust
but the man

survives.

STRIDE TOWARD FREEDOM

Stride Toward Freedom is all about walking. In his twenties, Martin Luther King, Jr. arrived in Montgomery, Alabama with his new wife, Coretta Scott King, and his new doctorate from Boston University. He took the pulpit of the Dexter Avenue Baptist Church in 1954. Knowing he needed pastoral experience, he immersed himself into the life of the Dexter Avenue Church. On December 1, 1955, Rosa Parks was arrested on a city bus and his life would never be the same.

Soon after Parks' arrest, the Black ministers of Montgomery decided to embark on a boycott of the city buses. They formed the Montgomery Improvement Association and elected the young Martin King as their president. The Montgomery Bus Protest, as Dr. King called it, which required intricate and devoted organization, lasted just over a year.

Dr. King published *Stride Toward Freedom* in 1958, just two years after the conclusion of the bus protest. He was young and his writing was too. The prose in *Stride Toward Freedom* is driven by events, the walking—the strides—which resulted in integrated buses in Montgomery, Alabama.

Christology

"It was Jesus of Nazareth that stirred the Negroes."
Stride Toward Freedom, p. 71

The white people often say
I'm stirring people up,

causing a ruckus where
there was no ruckus before

I came. It might seem
that way to them

because they have never been
at a Negro family's dinner

table. They have never
tasted the angry exhaustion

that lives on this side of town.
They have never sat in

Rev. Abernathy's church. They
have never heard him preach the

Jesus he knows. The leper-touching
Jesus. The cheek-turning Jesus.

The enemy-loving Jesus.
That's the ruckus. It's a holy ruckus

and Jesus brought it,
not me.

Real Peace

"...you have never had real peace in Montgomery."
Stride Toward Freedom, p. 27

We're just trying
not to fight.

Just trying to pay
the bills, the house note,

the way forward.
Don't think

that just because
my wife takes time

with her hat and gloves,
that we are

as satisfied as you,
because we are

ready to take off
hats and gloves

and walk your city
to a grinding, jarring

halt.

Highway Robbery

"Negroes paid their fares at the front door and were forced to get off and reboard the bus at the rear. Often the bus pulled off with the Negroes' dime in the box before he had time to reach the rear door."
Stride Toward Freedom, p. 28

Ain't that somethin'?
When bus exhaust fumes

swirl around my head
and the bus' metal side

laughs on its way,
I stand still, wondering

if the bus driver will
look at his childrens'

eyes tonight at supper,
sit on the front porch

as they play on the grass.
When they plead

to go for ice cream
will he smile a dime

into their giggling
hands?

Tired

"...tired feet for tired souls."
Stride Toward Freedom, p. 54

These feet slip between sheets
to a morning floor.

Before coffee & language
they know the air,

they welcome sock
and shoe.

Laces hold them
ready for the work

of the day,
of being beneath.

They create the straight
way of sidewalk,

the step of curb,
the caution of cross

walk, the patience
of standing still.

When heel and arch
and toe press

leather to concrete
they scuff

the smile of protest,
the unmistakable joy

of defiance.

Men Were Seen

"Men were seen riding mules to work..."
Stride Toward Freedom, p. 42

Go 'head and call us
"country."

My overalls can't hear
you and if they did

they wouldn't care.
Calluses don't lie.

These work shoes,
all leather and barn,

see perfectly well what's
in front of them.

There is sky today
seeing us all.

We been ready
for this denim.

These hands been hard
long as they been black.

Domestics

"I knew that the South Jackson line, which ran past our house, carried more Negro passengers than any other line in Montgomery, and that this first bus was usually filled with domestic workers going to their jobs."
Stride Toward Freedom, p. 41

Domestic workers are up
early. I know this.

I've seen them sitting erect
in this bus: hair, dresses, coats,

collars, ties perfect, armoring
themselves for another day,

hoping humility won't fester
into humiliation, setting

the worries of their own
families to the side,

preparing to care about
the worries of a white

family who will call them
by their first names.

This bus slows, stops, hums,
then growls back to speed.

The domestics stare straight
ahead, only breathing in.

The Day of Days

"The Day of Days, December 5"
Stride Toward Freedom, p. 41

You plan and call and organize
and prepare for every eventuality

but you never know what will come.
"My wife and I woke earlier than usual"

and I was afraid. I was still saying
"if we could get 60%" I would be

satisfied. In my mind, buses rolled
by with Black people atop the bus

and hanging from windows, dragging
their feet. White men and women

filled the bus laughing, doubled-
over laughing. What was I

thinking would happen?
"I was in the kitchen" whispering

over a cup of coffee when
I heard Coretta cry "Martin, Martin,

come quickly." I stopped praying
and ran into the living room

breathing like an army.
"A slowly moving bus" rolled

down our street like a hearse,
the casket still years away.

Coretta sang into my faithlessness,
"Darling, it's empty." I could

hardly believe it. Sometimes
believing and knowing have to

happen at the same time.

One Arrest

"...the police succeeded in making one arrest."
Stride Toward Freedom, p. 43

Home from college for Christmas Break
he saw an "elderly woman" on the corner

hesitant to step into the street,
unsure of the concrete, the cars,

the color of safety constantly changed.
She leaned like one who needed

to cross. She looked in more directions
than there were. He walked up

behind her, spoke to her. She took his arm
like the prophet's staff it was,

raised her eyes and stepped
into the street. Her brown-heeled shoe

greeting the concrete with a firmness
of its own making. She did not

look down. She thanked him
at the opposite curb. They smiled

until the police walked up. He urged
her to go on. She refused.

The police said words they would not
say to their grandmothers.

She told them she'd been scared
to cross but this young man—

so they arrested him for intimidating
passengers. She recorded his face

in her mind and kept it there for
years after. An icon. Almost

a saviour.

Mass Meetings

"We are here this evening..."
Stride Toward Freedom, p. 50

These meetings were our lungs.
Here we breathed.

We needed to christen
an organization, a leader.

I didn't know these people.
Abernathy was my only

friend. We baptized ourselves
the Montgomery Improvement

Association, a name as good as any
other. Better than one

that sounded too much like
their White Citizen Councils.

They were named for terror.
We were named for resurrection.

Then it was me. Put the new
guy out there. He hasn't been

beaten by them yet. He has
a degree of distance that

will throw them for a bit.
My only real qualification:

I didn't yet know
the density of the human

fist.

Our Names

"We'd better decide now if we're going to be fearless men or scared boys."
Stride Toward Freedom, p. 46

Some thought we should conceal
the leaders' names.

I thought so too,
at first.

But a wise man stopped
us from making this

error. Who are you?
He urged us to the light.

Who are you? Was just
the right question.

Its answer would be
known in time.

I have never been
fearless. I have once

been a boy.
I will never be fearless.

But I will always be
a man.

Refusal

"…a righteous man has no alternative but to refuse to cooperate with an evil system. This I felt was the nature of our action. I conceived of our movement as an act of massive noncooperation. From then on, I rarely used the word 'boycott.'"
Stride Toward Freedom, p. 39

To see it. To know its
brutality. Its taste.

This raises the sour water
in the back of the throat.

This tingles the fingertips,
compels a choice.

The shoulders straighten,
arms loosen, stance widens,

breathing eases.
There are a million ways

to say no.

Hate Meets Love

"To meet hate with retaliatory hate would do nothing but intensify the existence of evil in the universe. Hate begets hate; violence begets violence; toughness begets a greater toughness. We must meet the forces of hate with the power of love..."
Stride Toward Freedom, p. 74

1

Here is a chemistry
lost to most

humans. We think anger
is best drowned

in a victor's grin, a smile
that whispers

in the language death speaks.
This chemistry feels

good and it feels nothing
at the same time.

This thinking boils
human grievance into

a poison stew, a lunch
of flesh.

2

Imagine instead, a slowness,
my own breath. Exactly like

the breath of the one
I think I hate.

Faith

"...I believe that there is a creative personal power in the universe who is the ground and essence of all reality—a power that cannot be explained in materialistic terms."
Stride Toward Freedom, p. 79

Is hard. Is a tribe
of questions. I want

to learn its language,
to speak

with its citizens. I want
to live beside them

but I am the son
of questions. I cannot

abandon my uncertain
family.

I have chosen
to be faithful to them.

I hope they let me live
near the God

who gave me the mind
to ask them.

This God surely cannot
fear a question

from my threat-less head.
This creative God

could surely rewrite
my questions into a poem

less blasphemous
than my night prayers.

Be Broken

"...nonviolent resistance was one of the most potent weapons
available to oppressed people in their quest for social justice."
Stride Toward Freedom, p. 89

When the hand
scoops salt water and pours

it over the head, it is a baptism
in walking forward, an admission

that the eyes are in the front
of the human

head. They see in
one direction. They see

a lunch counter
become an altar.

Food and hatred can both be
thrown at people.

Both feed the one
who throws them.

The blood streaming
from a human head

consecrates the plates
and coffee cups onto which it

spills. But the human head needs
no consecration.

Its sanctity is proven
by the fact that it can

bleed.

Cowardice

"…not a method for cowards."
Stride Toward Freedom, p. 90

We need to be friends
with the cowards who hate

us and we need to love
the cowardice right out

of them. That is how
we love the cowardice

out of ourselves
at the same time.

So much harder to tighten
the human hand

into a rose
than a fist.

<u>Because</u>

"…nonviolent resistance is a willingness to accept suffering without retaliation…'Rivers of blood may have to flow before we gain our freedom, but it must be our blood,' Gandhi said to his countrymen."
Stride Toward Freedom, p. 91

Because then there will be
no doubt.

Because then it will be
ours.

Because then we will have
earned it.

Because no one gives up
power.

Because the rose crushed
is still a rose.

Because being human
is a choice.

Because some choose it
everyday.

Because some do
not.

Because some are
willing.

Because blood doesn't
mean you're alive.

Because "This is my blood"
is still true.

Because "This is my blood"
has always been

true.

Inheritance

"The nonviolent resister not only refuses to shoot his opponent
but he also refuses to hate him. At the center of nonviolence
stands the principle of love."
Stride Toward Freedom, p. 92

That angry voice on the phone
was once someone's dearest

baby. A most promising little boy
who said: "Listen n*****, we've taken

all we want from you; before next
week you'll be sorry you ever came

to Montgomery." This beautiful
little boy smiling, giggling, today

sings out a hatred he has learned.
A song his country handed him.

His hatred and fear are not really
his. He inherited them. He took

them into himself without
knowing how gruesome they

would taste, how they would
sicken him too.

I cannot hate him
for inheriting this. I will not

destroy him just because
someone taught him

to destroy me.

A Wind

"...the universe is on the side of justice. Consequently, the believer in nonviolence has deep faith in the future."
Stride Toward Freedom, p. 95

Even the clouds paid attention
when we stopped riding the buses.

They could see us, through
their shifting eyes,

eyes the color of "No."
They urged us in a voice

soft as God's, in a language
native and familiar as the blue

of sky. They knew
we would walk. They knew

we would wear out shoes.
They pushed us even,

with their spirit breath. They
urged us with a wind

we could not see.

Bomb

"After putting the baby to bed, Coretta and Mrs. Williams went
to the living room to look at television. About nine-thirty they
heard a noise in front that sounded as though someone had
thrown a brick. In a matter of seconds an explosion rocked the
house. A bomb had gone off on the porch."
Stride Toward Freedom, p. 125

War is like this: two women,
a baby, a man gone, a man lost.

I was lost like this: a baby
in the back bedroom,

a wife shaking, unable to be
still. A friend, calm but about

to break.

A crowd gathered. I ran home
to see what was left of me.

The crowd was angry.
I wanted their anger

to love my own. But my wife's
shaking stopped, keeping me

from breaking.

Keeping me from becoming
the bomb I feared.

Midnight

"Coretta had already fallen asleep and just as I was about to doze off the telephone rang. An angry voice said 'Listen, n*****, we've taken all we want from you; before next week you'll be sorry you ever came to Montgomery.'"

"In this state of exhaustion, when my courage had all but gone, I decided to take my problem to God. With my head in my hands... I spoke...' I have nothing left. I've come to the point where I can't face it alone.'"
Stride Toward Freedom, p. 125

I have always been
here. In this midnight

kitchen. In this midnight
city. In this midnight

life. I have always known
this is when

the strength comes. In this
midnight country.

In my midnight throat.
From this midnight

God.

This Day

"Before I could get these words out, Rex Thomas—a reporter
for the Associated Press—came up to me with a paper in his
hand. 'Here is the decision that you have been waiting for. Read
this release.'"
Stride Toward Freedom, p. 152

Sometimes, when you least expect it,
you are able

to exhale. You know you will
breathe in again, and you live

in hope that another chance to breathe
out will come in your lifetime.

This day the air was free.
This day the air looked up

at me from the sidewalk. I thought
it smiled, even. This day

tasted clean. This day was all
sky. This day would become

a birth. But my awe wouldn't
let me consider that for more

than a moment because this day was
light and darkness. This day

was morning and night
in their created order.

Sheet, Cross, and Flame

"That night the Ku Klux Klan rode. The radio had announced their plan to demonstrate throughout the Negro community, and threats of violence and new bombings were in the air."
Stride Toward Freedom p. 155

They are always the most cruel
when they lose.

The sheet, the cross, the flame
are most sour

when their lie slips away.
It's because they've convinced

themselves of their own
story, of their own need.

The sheet, the cross, the flame
can only hide

for so long. They hang
on clotheslines, atop

their churches, just under
their tongues.

It's hard to live
with a flame under

your tongue.

When a Church Burns

"We finally learned that besides Ralph's home and church, Bob
Graetz's home and three other Baptist churches—Bell Street,
Hutchinson Street, and Mt. Olive—had all been hit."
Stride Toward Freedom, pp. 166-167

When a church burns
the body leans away

from the cross,
letting the weight

of crucifixion do
its work.

The lungs believe
they will fill

with air again but
this is heresy.

The nails create
a weeping pain,

the pierced feet
pull, in an effort

to save their own
skin. But it is

the whole body
that kills. Its

muscle and bone-
weight droop

toward an unused
tomb. Not far away,

a man grins. He
has fingers like

matches, a tongue the
color of gasoline.

He believes his hands
smell like history,

while the flames in his
eyes take the shape of

his country.

<u>Tears</u>

"Discouraged, and still revolted by the bombings, for some strange reason I began to feel a personal sense of guilt for everything that was happening. In this mood I went to the mass meeting on Monday. There for the first time, I broke down in public."
Stride Toward Freedom, p. 169

It's like Jesus
touched my face

with wet fingers. It's like
the whole country needed

what I couldn't stop
in front of hundreds

of people. It's like

the warm wood of the church
opened me. It's like

the man in the gospel story
whose blindness is cured

when Jesus rubs water
and dust, mud, into his eyes.

It's like I was that
man. It's like the mud

was made from my own
tears. It's like

I was that broken.

Smoldering

"The same morning an unexploded bomb, crudely assembled
from 12 sticks of dynamite, was found still smoldering on my
porch."
Stride Toward Freedom, p. 170

The language spoken
by "an unexploded bomb"

is the language of possibility.
It is a terror tongue,

it sounds like a silent infant,
still forever. It echoes

like a still woman,
silent on the floor of her own

home. It is where they wait
for father and husband.

Home is where the heart
breaks into pieces the size

of privilege. Is it my good
luck that twelve sticks

of dynamite did not sing
the chorus they were taught?

Is it my good fortune
that a fuse doesn't always

complete its work?

Here is America's truth:

this bomb was not
the only thing smoldering

in my home.

We Prepared

"On December 20, the bus integration order finally reached
Montgomery. A mass meeting was immediately scheduled for
that evening, to give people final instructions before returning
to the buses the following day."
Stride Toward Freedom, p. 160

You'd think we were
on another planet,

the order took so long
to reach us. Washington, D.C.

to Montgomery is eight-hundred miles,
five states. But we prepared.

We were ready to be
gracious. We know

how they are when they lose.
"At St. John A.M.E. Church

I read the following message…
'For more than twelve months

now, we the Negro citizens…
more honorable to walk in

dignity than ride in humiliation…
these twelve months have not been

easy…agony and darkness of Good
Friday…but…truth crushed

to earth will rise again.'"
We have not been victorious

over anyone. We want to ride
beside everyone.

Coretta Scott King: Montgomery

If there is sheet music
for this city I have never

seen its likes before. The
melody keeps changing.

Just as I start to sing one
line I see the notes

at the end of the line
dodging and ducking

in every direction.
Quarter notes dart

from their place
on the staff and try

to stand up taller,
to puff out their chests

like whole notes, keeping
the voice alive longer.

I can sing almost
anything but this

shape-shifting opera
of shoes makes it

hard to breathe. It keeps
moving from solo

to choral piece. I know
there are other voices

and I know their timbre
is all shoe and sweat

but I fear they will
leave me

bare.

WHY WE CAN'T WAIT

Why We Can't Wait explores the dramatic and tragic events of 1963. Dr. King knew this year was a pivotal one, not only in the life of the Civil Rights Movement, but in the life of the nation. In August 1963, the nation's hopes soared with the March on Washington, at which Dr. King delivered his famous "I Have a Dream" speech. But just two weeks later in Birmingham Alabama, four little girls were killed in the bombing of the 16th Street Baptist Church, and two boys were shot and killed on the same Sunday. In November of 1963, the nation mourned the assassination of President John F. Kennedy. Also in 1963, Dr. King wrote "The Letter from Birmingham Jail," perhaps the most important work of protest literature ever written. Dr. King has four children and is 34 years old as he writes this book. He has seen far more violence than when he wrote *Stride Toward Freedom*. *Why We Can't Wait* seeks to explain the urgency of the moment. Its blunt and impatient title shows us how Dr. King was feeling.

<u>1963</u>

"It is the beginning of the year of our Lord 1963. I see a young Negro boy. He is sitting on a stoop in front of a vermin-infested apartment house in Harlem. The stench of garbage is in the halls...I see a young Negro girl. She is sitting on the stoop of a rickety wooden one-family house in Birmingham. Some visitors would call it a shack."
Why We Can't Wait, p. xi

1

A boy sits on his stoop.
The house leans hopeless

as he is. The rats love him
and his family. They know

him. He has nowhere
to go. He has nowhere

to be. He dreams of nowhere.
When he wakes after

dreams of nowhere he goes
nowhere. His school

forgets him. He forgets him.
His parents work but

their exhaustion forgets
him too. Is he a dream?

Has his country deferred
him? Can nowhere

explode?

2

A girl sits on her stoop.
The wood of her home

older than her grandmother,
but not as sturdy.

The field where her parents
work is thirsty as she

is, but not as angry.
She sits and remembers

school but learns now
in a field because debts

are loud. They shout,
more fury than books.

3

This is the year
young people will sing

fury in a melody
that hurts, in a rhythm

that burns. A flame so hot
fire hoses shove these

singers against walls.
But those hoses and their

water, their judges,
their county clerks,

their governor and their
country cannot extinguish

anything.

Late

"The pale history books in Harlem and Birmingham told how the nation had fought a war over slavery, Abraham Lincoln had signed a document that would come to be known as the Emancipation Proclamation. The war had been won but not a just peace. Equality had never arrived. Equality was a hundred years late."
Why We Can't Wait, p. xiii

Late is never.
This is why we can't.

A hundred years does not
taste like late.

It tastes like forgotten.
It looks like never

happened. This is why
children sang their way

into jail. This is how
a country moves

forward. By burning
itself on its own

summer.

Below the Surface

"Explosively, America's third revolution had begun—the Negro Revolution—had begun. For the first time in the long and turbulent history of the nation, almost one thousand cities were engulfed in civil turmoil, with violence trembling just below the surface."
Why We Can't Wait, p. 2

If you cut human skin
with a sharp enough blade,

the very second you slice
into it, blood fills

the space the blade created.
The red life oozes

forth, a rhythm of replacement,
a falsehood. The split skin

only looks red. This is
blood. This is broken

skin. This is America's
weeping. Human blood

bubbling forth from
vein, onto skin, and streaking

down the arm or leg
or forehead, it becomes

a map documenting
precisely where the country

refuses to go.

The Only Power

"When for decades you have been able to make a man compromise his manhood by threatening him with a cruel and unjust punishment, and when suddenly he turns upon you and says" 'Punish me. I do not deserve it. But because I do not deserve it, I will accept it so that the world will know that I am right and you are wrong.'"
Why We Can't Wait, p. 21

When a person accepts
undeserved suffering

a spark bursts into air.
It coughs, gasps

and breathes. It begins
its burning life.

When a person accepts
undeserved suffering

the privilege of the mighty
trembles before the only

power it does not have:
the willingness to suffer.

We

"The religious tradition of the Negro had shown him that the nonviolent resistance of early Christians had constituted a moral offensive of such overriding power that it shook the Roman Empire."
Why We Can't Wait, p. 30

When one piece of the machine
slows and stops

the whole machine might
slow and stop.

This truth lies buried
in the love affair

between part and whole.
If I, if you, then eventually

we. If he and she,
then over time we.

It has always been
this way.

Gandhi knew when one
man walked to the sea

he would attract another
and when two walked

to the sea, the salt would
eventually be free.

When one decided
to march, eventually

one thousand decided
to march and they became

the salt.

Eye to Eye

"The striking thing about the nonviolent crusade of 1963 was
that so few felt the sting of bullets…Looking back, it becomes
obvious that the oppressors were restrained not only because
the world was looking but also because, standing before them,
were hundreds, sometimes thousands, of Negroes who for the
first time dared to look back at a white man, eye to eye."
Why We Can't Wait, p. 34

This is the glance
I never dared. These

are the words
the glance spoke:

I am a man. I will not
look at my shoes

anymore. I will
square my shoulders.

The bones within are
the same as yours.

The same but for
one difference:

my bones know how
to carry your dying

privilege.

Startling

"If you had visited Birmingham before the third of April in the one-hundredth anniversary year of the Negro's emancipation, you might have come to a startling conclusion."
Why We Can't Wait, p. 44

Nothing changed. The ink
on Lincoln's proclamation

was still wet. It waited
like a tear. It was not dry.

It sat on the paper
for a century. What rain

lasts a century? What blood
takes more than a hundred

years to dry? This waiting
has stood up slowly

but it stands now. It looks
you in the eye and

spits the word: *Today.*

One Black Woman

"One of the city commissioners, a member of the body that ruled municipal affairs, would be Eugene 'Bull' Connor, a racist who prided himself on knowing how to handle the Negro and keep him in his 'place.'"
Why We Can't Wait, p. 47

He must have learned
these lessons he claimed

from ancestors and teachers
who lived with the same

fear. Is a demon passed on
from father to son

by blood, by spit?
He received this demon

somehow. He sharpened it.
He did not fear it until

one Black woman stood
before him, looking

straight at him for just
a few seconds that lasted

a thousand years.

There Is One

"In Birmingham, one of the nation's most courageous freedom fighters, the Reverend Fred Shuttlesworth, had organized the Alabama Christian Movement for Human Rights."
Why We Can't Wait, p. 49

Often behind a great moment
is one, in this case, man.

One man who could
see the sky before it could be

pierced. One man who could
imagine a city unlike

the one where he lived. A city
where skin, Black as a

white man's fear, could
sing a melody so haunting

even the ghosts would run
scared for their lives.

This man could hear
the song's conclusion

while singing its opening
lines. He could anticipate

where he would need
to breathe so he would

have enough air for the song
that rang like jail.

He became a whole note,
singing the melody

of steel. The harmony
of cell doors the world

thought were slamming
shut. He knew better:

their metal doors only seemed
to close. These jail cells

were filled with fire
and fire is always

free.

When Children Sing

"I have stood in a meeting with hundreds of youngsters and joined in while they sang 'Aint Gonna Let Nobody Turn Me 'Round.' It is not just a song; it is a resolve. A few minutes later, I have seen those same youngsters refuse to turn around from the onrush of a police dog..."
Why We Can't Wait, p. 64

How does a song work
like this?

How does music
face a snarling

dog? When children
sing, their skin

strengthens into a soul.
When the police

let loose an angry dog
their skin breaks

from within. The country's
wound has just begun

to bleed, while these singing
children redeem us all.

It Takes Time

"We made it clear that we would not send anyone out to demonstrate who had not convinced himself and us that he could accept and endure violence without retaliating."
Why We Can't Wait, p. 65

It takes time
to learn this.

It must be proven
in the light

of day. That you
will look him

in the hand
and love his fist

to death.

Commandment Number One: Meditate daily on the teachings
and life of Jesus.

Meditate Daily

What this does.
When Jesus is

a needle that gets under
the skin.

It must break the skin
and once it does, it

cuts what is there
into pieces of the past.

This needle
of God.

This savior who stabs
his way into us,

who slaughters us
into salvation.

Commandment Number Two: Remember always that the nonviolent movement in Birmingham seeks justice and reconciliation—not victory.

<u>Remembering</u>

Remembering is
the challenge.

We want to return
to the way

things should be.
Even if they have

never been.

Commandment Number Three: Walk and talk in the manner of love, for God is love.

In The Manner

It's imitation,
this faith.

It's trying to be
like—

this love, this God.
To be like

does not require
losing one's own.

It only requires
desire.

Commandment Number Four: Pray daily to be used by God in order that all men might be free.

Being

To be of
use.

To be for
others

is the only
being

that is
of use.

Commandment Number Five: Sacrifice personal wishes in order that all men might be free.

Setting Aside

Setting aside
the personal.

Calling out
wishes for what

they are.

Making space
for another.

For a multitude
of others.

For a multitude
so large

it holds everyone
and is everyone.

Commandment Number Six: Observe with both friend and foe the ordinary rules of courtesy.

The Ordinary Rules

If only they were
ordinary.

If only they were
rules.

If only they could
be observed,

enacted in flesh,
breathed into

blood, worked
into hands.

Commandment Number Seven: Seek to perform regular service for others and for the world.

<u>Outward</u>

Because our eyes
look outward

we can see
others, the world

that holds them,
the largeness

of the possible.

When our eyes
only see what is

within, we miss
the beautiful

other. We miss
ourselves.

Commandment Number Eight: Refrain from the violence of fist, tongue, or heart.

Weapons

We have a mighty
arsenal.

We are so good
at destruction:

a fist, a word,
a silent hatred.

All can be
fatal.

All destroy:
the wounded and

the wound-er,
equally dead.

Commandment Number Nine: Strive to be in good spiritual and bodily health.

<u>Because</u>

Because the soul speaks
at the tips of the fingers.

Because the conscience forms
words that fall from human lips.

Because grace builds
on the body.

Commandment Number Ten: Follow the directions of the movement and of the captain on a demonstration.

She Knows

She knows
what is around the corner.

She knows the police
have nails

in their nightsticks.
She knows

when you are too far
to run back

to the church.
You are a part

of the movement.
You are not the movement.

Listen to her.

The Ten Commandments of Nonviolence Pledge Card asked participants for the name and address of their "Nearest Relative."

This Truth

There is no maybe
in this.

Only will.
Some of us will

die in this work.
In truth, all

of us will.
The only uncertainty

is where, when,
and how.

Once I befriended
this truth

I became
myself.

When You Focus

"By the end of the first three days of lunch-counter sit-ins, there had been thirty-five arrests…Something was happening to the Negro in this city, just as something revolutionary was taking place in the mind, heart, and soul of Negroes all over America."
Why We Can't Wait, p. 75

When you not only
hear the curses

but also feel their saliva
land on your ear.

When the pouring
of scrambled eggs and hot gravy

on your head is
the easiest insult

to bear. When you
focus on an old hymn

your mother sang
at her sink

so you do not hear
the poisoned words

they hiss at you.
They may think

they degrade me.
But I am taller

than I have ever been.

Martin King Speaks of Ralph Abernathy

"I pulled off my shirt and pants, got into work clothes and went back to the other room to tell them I had decided to go to jail. 'I do not know what will happen…But I have to make a faith act.'"

I turned to Ralph Abernathy.

'I know you want to be in your pulpit on Easter Sunday, Ralph. But I am asking you to go with me.'"
Why We Can't Wait, p. 81

I knew what he would say
before I asked him.

But asking is my religion.
He shook his head and

smiled, like he always does.
He spoke in the language

of brother. In the dialect
of love. He knew

the buoyancy of a decision
made. He knew I did too.

Once you say it,
the doing is easier.

Once you do it,
your body floats

into prayer.

The Father I Wanted to Be

"When I left my Atlanta home some days before, my wife,
Coretta, had just given birth to our fourth child."
Why We Can't Wait, p. 83

I am not the father
I wanted to be.

I am not the husband
I promised to be.

I am only trying
to be the man

I am called to be.
Coretta, thank God,

is the rock and sky,
the mother and wife

she is called
to be.

He Was Baptized Ralph

"I had never been truly in solitary confinement; God's companionship does not stop at the door of a jail cell."
Why We Can't Wait, p. 84

I am sure
God looks like

a certain Baptist minister
with a lined face,

rivers of worry
have washed

his skin for decades.
He is old

and Black.
He preaches

in Montgomery.
He was baptized

Ralph and he stands
beside me

today. He is the laughing
presence my whole

world needs.

Even Though

"In any nonviolent campaign there are four basic steps: collection of the facts to determine whether injustices exist; negotiation; self-purification; and direct action. We have gone through these steps in Birmingham." From "Letter from Birmingham Jail" in *Why We Can't Wait,* p. 87

We must know
what we do.

We must think through
the consequences

of what they do to us,
of what we might do

to them. We must be
as close to pure

as humans come.
We must walk straight

into their arms.

They Can't Help Themselves

"We know through painful experience that freedom is never
voluntarily given by the oppressor; it must be demanded by the
oppressed."
"Letter from Birmingham Jail" in *Why We Can't Wait,* p. 91

They can't help themselves.
And that's not just a way of saying it.

They truly cannot help themselves.
We have to love their hatred

out of them. They cannot
see it. They do not think

it even exists.
We must help them to

be human, to be decent.
Our marching, our nights

in jail, our aching bruises
will help them,

will save them.

A Legal Theory

"Any law that uplifts human personality is just. Any law that degrades human personality is unjust."
"Letter from Birmingham Jail" in *Why We Can't Wait*, p. 94

Here is a legal theory
most bar associations

do not know. This
context. This landscape.

The law lives
in a world with people.

And people use stones
against one another.

So laws keep us
from our animal selves.

But laws can also
urge us deeper

into our animal selves.
We cling to anything

that "uplifts" the real.
We protest all that

"degrades." This
law keeps us

human.

When Discomfort Is a Creed

"Oppressed people cannot remain oppressed forever."
"Letter from Birmingham Jail" in *Why We Can't Wait,* p. 101

When discomfort is
a creed I believe.

When urgency is
a sacrament.

When insistence makes
you holy.

When impatience saves
you,

along with the whole
waiting world.

We Hardly Know Each Other

"I have been greatly disappointed with the white church and its
leadership…all too many others have been more cautious than
courageous and have remained silent behind the anesthetizing
security of stained-glass windows."
"Letter from Birmingham Jail" in *Why We Can't Wait,* p. 104

Sometimes it seems
we hardly know each other.

The same cross
floats above their church.

The same savior
does the same saving.

But they make prudence
a grand virtue

when prudence is a good
little virtue.

Like they have all the time
in their world.

Like they can afford
to wait.

Not when four
girls die at Sunday School.

Not when a boy's bicycle
becomes his cross.

In Dresses and Bows

"Jim Bevel had the inspiration of setting a 'D' Day, when the students would go to jail in historic numbers. When that day arrived, young people converged on the Sixteenth Street Baptist Church in wave after wave… there were 2,500 demonstrators in jail at one time…"
Why We Can't Wait, p. 117

In dresses and bows.
In jeans and t-shirts.

In crisp church shirts
and skinny black ties.

With songs and laughter.
With swagger and sweat.

For honor and for fun.
For a future they wanted.

For a present they refused.

A Crucifixion

"The newspapers of May 4 carried pictures of prostrate women, and policemen bending over them with raised clubs; of children marching up to the bared fangs of police dogs; of the terrible force of pressure hoses sweeping bodies into the streets."
Why We Can't Wait, p. 118

1

A crucifixion does not
always require a cross.

It sometimes takes the shape
of a sidewalk, a cop, a night

stick raised, blooming with nails.
A crucifixion does not

need Roman soldiers.
It sometimes only needs

a fearful uniformed man
whose fear poses as anger,

a fear he doesn't even know
he has.

2

When a police dog bares
its teeth and lunges

it is best to live in another
country, in another time.

When that dog's collar
barely controls him,

when its handler smiles
at you, terrified,

you see how many songs
are required.

3

When a high-pressure hose
hits you from a few yards

away, bones fail. You can't
hear them but you feel

them. And you collapse
in a bloodless defeat.

But not a defeat.
Because fear is not

the only terrible force.

Water

"On one of these days, when the pressure in Connor's hoses was so high that it peeled the bark off the trees, Fred Shuttlesworth was hurled by a blast of water against the side of a building. Suffering injuries in his chest, he was carried away in an ambulance. Connor, when told, responded in characteristic fashion. 'I wish he'd been carried away in a hearse,' he said."
Why We Can't Wait, p. 124

Some people
come willingly

to be baptized.
Some welcome

the water and its danger-
ous promise.

Some people
let the baptismal

flood carry them
from the present they know

well, to a future they have
not seen.

My Brother's Keeper

"Following a Ku Klux Klan meeting on the outskirts of town,
the home of my brother, the Reverend A. D. King, was bombed."
Why We Can't Wait, p. 127

I am, of course,
my brother's keeper.

I have always been
my brother's keeper.

We have always been
our brothers' keepers.

His home is our home.
The bomb on his porch

is the bomb on our porch.
The men who leave

the bomb in the darkness,
they are ours too.

The Height of A. Philip Randolph

"The dean of Negro leaders, A. Philip Randolph… proposed a March on Washington to unite in one luminous action all of the forces from the far-flung front."
Why We Can't Wait, p. 149

Sometimes a tall man
has the answer.

This man has worked
on enough trains

to know the meaning
of departure,

the taste of arrival.
He stands, closer

to God than most
of us. He hears

the clouds whisper
what can only be

heard from a height:
march.

A Waning Crescent

*On 9/15/1963 the moon over Birmingham, Alabama was a
waning crescsent, only 6% visible. For Addie Mae Collins, Cynthia
Wesley, Denise McNair, Carole Robertson, Johnny Robinson, and
Virgil Ware*

You were a waning
crescent, the barest
of slivers in the darkest
night Alabama knows.

You were a trace
of light
these children could not
see.

They each slept
under your curving
back, unaware of the
tides to come.

You were a silent wound
in the stabbed sky.
You said nothing.

You should have been
a warning to us all
on such a lightless night
as 1963.

The bomber, the cop,
the boy, the bricks, the bullets,
they did not ask
for your light.

They did not need
your protection.

But we do.
We need to see.
We need to be
the waning, the waxing,
and the warning.

Our Lady of Sorrows Comes to Birmingham 2

"On one horror-filled September morning they blasted the lives
from four innocent girls studying in their Sunday-school class.
Police killed another child in the streets, and hate-filled white
youths climaxed the day with a wanton murder of a Negro boy
harmlessly riding his bicycle."
Why We Can't Wait, p. 136

for Virgil Ware

A boy on his bike
should be out of bounds.

Dreaming of his paper
route. Admiring his

big brother. Smiling
til his cheek turns.

His mother waited
for him. Doted on him.

Treated him like
the little one he was.

This moment, a
wound riding by on a motorbike,

would break her too.
She would stand beside

this cross and stare
at what their fear does.

She would breathe
without wanting to.

She would open her arms
to receive the altar

of his limp body.
She would raise him

to the God who did not
protect him. She would

hiss through her bruised
teeth:

"This is my body, given
up for you."

This November

"The assassination of President Kennedy killed not only a man but a complex of illusions. It demolished the myth that hate and violence can be confined in an airtight chamber to be employed against but a few."
Why We Can't Wait, p. 179

I wish I could believe
in fairy tales, in Santa Claus,

in a tooth fairy, a rabbit
heralding Easter.

But this November wind
unmasks everything.

This is our country. This
assassin's republic,

this shame that shoots
from an empty warehouse

window, this spitting land
with more than enough

bullets for us all.

His Fist
In Selma, Alabama, January 18, 1965

"King's attacker in the lobby of the Hotel Albert was a gaunt-faced white man with a stubble of beard. He was identified as Jimmy George Robinson, 26, a member of the National States Rights Party...Robinson who had spoken to King earlier in the day, said he wanted to talk to him again. 'What do you want?' King replied. Without a word, Robinson threw a right that struck King solidly on the right temple...John Lewis, chairman of the Student Nonviolent Coordinating Committee, pinned Robinson's arms."
From the *Chicago Tribune*, January 19, 1965

I never saw it
coming. In the lobby

of a hotel,
of all places.

He didn't even face
me. I never saw

his fist, backed
by a city, a state,

a republic of refusal,
a land of "know

your place." His fist
fanged my temple

like a snake I had
not seen. I knew right then

I'd break. But he'd break
too, like a law,

like a country.

Coretta Scott King: 1963

We have daughters now. Girl
humans, in this year of girls.

Girls in church basements,
wandering the streets at night

wondering why their childhoods
were stolen by their country.

This is also the year of learning,
a civics lesson I thought

I already knew: that Black
bodies mean nothing,

that Black bodies mean
everything. That Black

bodies still do not count
in America. I thought I knew

this. I must keep forgetting
since America feels the need

to keep teaching me
this in years, in numbers,

in bodies, in daughters,
in girls.

WHERE DO WE GO FROM HERE: CHAOS OR COMMUNITY?

The title of Dr. King's final book asks a question. It also offers two profoundly different answers. He writes *Where Do We Go from Here: Chaos or Community?* in 1967, the final year of his life. This book follows the Nobel Peace Prize, which he felt called his activism forth into more global concerns. This last book also follows the announcement of his public opposition to the war in Vietnam, which he made one year to the day before he would lose his life. In New York City's Riverside Church, on April 4, 1967, Dr. King delivered a meticulously crafted speech explaining the immorality of the Vietnam War. This speech caused many American political leaders, some civil rights leaders, and many others, to abandon him. By the time Dr. King writes this last book, he has lived with regular death threats for several years. *Where Do We Go from Here: Chaos or Community?* reveals more nuance, a more global vision, more urgency, even some sadness.

Riot

"...in Watts, young Negroes had exploded in violence. In an irrational burst of rage they had sought to say something, but the flames had blackened both themselves and their oppressors."
Where Do We Go from Here? p. 2

When your mouth tries
to form a word

and your hearer turns
away before you even

get it out.
When your mouth tries

to turn away
before outing its form.

When your word mouths
a try. When your

away turns even.
When your out gets

tried, your even
words. When your

city walks away shaking
its head.

Decency

"For the vast majority of white Americans, the past decade—
the first phase—had been a struggle to treat the Negro with a
degree of decency, not of equality."
Where Do We Go from Here? p. 3

I am glad of decency
but I will not die for it.

I appreciate manners
but no one suffers

for them. This has never
been about decency.

We have never demanded
manners. Never once

have manners made
us human.

Manners and decency
reach down and pat us

on the head. This is
about me grabbing

your hand demanding
you ask my permission

before you touch me.

The Flag

"There were twice as many Negroes as whites in combat in
Vietnam at the beginning of 1967..."
Where Do We Go from Here? p. 7

Sometimes math confuses
me. But these numbers make

a sense that is perfectly
odd.

The flag is sewn
onto the shoulder of my

uniform. The flag asks
for my allegiance.

The flag sings its anthem
and asks me to sing

along. But when I do
this math, I suddenly

forget the melody. I
suddenly remember

a song I heard in a
dream, a song people

who looked like me
sang in a field

they did not own.
I remember a song

I heard in Birmingham,
just over the howl

of dogs and hoses,
a song more true

than the colors on
this flag.

Ready

"A good many observers have remarked that if equality could
come at once the Negro would not be ready for it. I submit
that the white American is even more unprepared."
Where Do We Go from Here? p. 9

This just proves how
little you know

about us. If you had
not spent the last

hundred years making
sure we could not

live next door. If you
had not spent the last

fifty years making
sure we could not

attend the same school.
If you had not

spent the last twenty
years making sure

we could not vote,
you might know

what it means
to be ready. You

might know what
we know about

being ready.

Preparation

"Negroes hold only one key to the double lock of peaceful change. The other is in the hands of the white community."
Where Do We Go from Here? p. 22

Some tell me there is
no such thing as peaceful change.

That true change always sounds
like tearing, like paper

being ripped in two. But I have
never believed in paper.

I have believed in readying
myself and others through suffering

and we are ready.

These Colors

"When we heard that Meredith had been shot in the back only a day after he had begun his Freedom March through Mississippi, there was a momentary hush of anger and dismay throughout the room."
Where Do We Go from Here? p. 23

James was willing
to walk alone.

But no one with skin
the color of wood

should walk alone
in Mississippi.

This is a land of men
the color of cowardice.

This is a land of guns
the color of shadows.

These colors bloom
in Mississippi. These colors

are not strong enough
to walk alone.

These colors look
for a man's back.

The Fact of Contact

"A productive and happy life is not something that you find; it is something that you make. And so the ability of Negroes and whites to work together, to understand each other, will not be found ready made; it must be created by the fact of contact."
Where Do We Go from Here? p. 28

When you can sit
face to face.

When you can live
house to house.

When you can study
desk by desk.

When we see that
it is just us.

When we look into
the eyes of those

we fear. When we
listen to the stories

of those we think
we know.

Then we begin
the work of not

killing each other.

Power's Weakness

"It is necessary to understand that Black Power is a cry of disappointment."
Where Do We Go from Here? p. 33

Usually the loudest voice
is the wounded voice.

Anger is hurt, wrapped
in masculinity.

If it isn't named, it isn't
healed, it takes on

a new shape, it looks
more like a fist than a

hand. It sounds more
like a growl than a song.

It feels more like a slap
than an ache.

Love and Power

"What is needed is a realization that power without love is reckless and abusive and that love without power is sentimental and anemic. Power at its best is love implementing the demands of justice."
Where Do We Go from Here? p. 38

Love gets on its knees
and washes its friends'

feet. Power pushes the other
aside. Love listens without

speaking back. Power insists
on itself. Power is

fist and voice, boot and
gun. Love gazes, waits,

considers, shares.
Love asks. Power orders.

Joined, Love and Power
consecrate the only

communion. They become
bread and wine, brick

and stone with which
we build and feed

the World House.

The Response

"Darkness cannot drive out darkness: only light can do that. Hate cannot drive out hate: only love can do that. The beauty of nonviolence is that in its own way and in its own time it seeks to break the chain reaction of evil."
Where Do We Go from Here? p. 65

It is almost amusing
how quickly we reach

for the wrong tool.
It is almost understandable

how we get things so
wrong.

This man angers me
so I give him my anger.

This country refuses
me so I spit refusal back.

If just once, we could
offer the open hand,

we might surprise the one
who hates us into remembering

his own humanity.

The Bones

"The step backward has a new name today. It is called the "white backlash." But the white backlash is nothing new. It is the surfacing of old prejudices, hostilities, ambivalences that have always been there."
Where Do We Go from Here? p. 72

Every forward
has a backward.
We carry stones

in our pockets,
old as air.
We carry angers

under our tongues,
written in our
ancestors' language.

We carry a bag
of bones, dry
and brittle as

the century
they died in.
Why is it so

hard to put down
the bag? Let the
bones

rest.

Our Country

"This is white America's most urgent challenge today. If America is to respond creatively to the challenge, many individuals, groups, and agencies, must rise above the hypocrisies of the past and begin to take an immediate and determined part in changing the face of their nation."
Where Do We Go from Here? p. 90

We can admit our
country's errors and not

melt into nothing. We can
be truthful about

the cruelties in history
without becoming

the cruelties. We can
name and admit,

confess and praise
at the same time.

This is a step, difficult
enough.

From here we must
build. But only if

you want to build.
If we choose not

to build, there is another
way:

burn.

Before The Heart

"Touring Watts a few days after that nightmarish riot in 1965, Bayard Rustin, Andrew Young and I confronted a group of youngsters who said to us joyously, 'We won.'

We asked them: 'How can you say you won when thirty-four Negroes are dead and your community is destroyed, and whites are using the riot as an excuse for inaction?'

Their answer: 'We won because we made them pay attention to us.'"
Where Do We Go from Here? p. 120

Before the heart can give
itself to another,

the eyes have to see
the other.

This is our wound:
Blindness creates

cruelty.

You cannot set dogs
on humans unless

you do not see
them.

You cannot slam
the night stick

on a woman's back
unless you do not see

her.

Here is our wound:
until you see us

our country will only
speak

in the language
of dogs.

Imagine This

"The curse of poverty has no justification in our age. It is socially as cruel and blind as the practice of cannibalism at the dawn of civilization...The time has come for us to civilize ourselves by the total, direct, and immediate abolition of poverty."
Where Do We Go from Here? p. 175

Imagine this: we know
how to solve poverty.

We know that schools,
kindness, jobs, patience

can lead to peace in one
generation, sometimes

less, even. We know
this. We know exactly

how to do it.
But imagine this:

we choose not to.

Where

"We have inherited a large house, a great 'world house' in which we have to live together—black and white, Easterner and Westerner, Gentile and Jew, Catholic and Protestant, Muslim and Hindu—a family unduly separated in ideas, culture, and interest, who, because we can never again live apart, must learn somehow to live with each other in peace."
Where Do We Go from Here? p. 177

Where we sleep,
where we drink coffee

or tea in the morning.
Where we take our

toast and oranges.
Where we wash and

ready ourselves for the day.
Where we put on our

clothes for the day: trousers,
uniform, dress, coat,

sweater, socks, shoes,
sandals, gloves, and

hat. We do not live
apart. We are all here.

It is just us in this house
where we either live

or die.

Thunder

"The deep rumbling of discontent that we hear today is the thunder of disinherited masses, rising from the dungeons of oppression to the bright hills of freedom."
Where Do We Go from Here? p. 179

There is something
about thunder.

Why it frightens
children. Why

it makes grown
men and women

look up to the sky,
squinting, wondering

what tempest is
to come.

Discontent is a
dungeon, a jail cell

below the ground.
No one stays

there. We rise
through anger

and protest
to become a

rumbling. We run
to hills from which

we can see the land
around us.

This is our thunder:
we are the storm.

House

"The stability of the large world house which is ours will involve
a revolution of values to accompany the scientific and freedom
revolutions engulfing the earth. We must rapidly shift from a
'thing'-oriented society to a 'person'– oriented society."
Where Do We Go from Here? p. 196

Most think houses are built
with wood, stone, brick.

We have a house built
of protest and prayer,

standing up and sitting
down, police vans, fire

hoses, snarling dogs,
arrest warrants. This

house is ours now if
we choose to build it.

We do so choose.

We build this house
by loving those who live

within it. There is nothing
about the house itself

to love. It is only we
who can love. It is only

the human inhabitants
of the house who can be

loved. It is only
we who can build.

If we so choose.

The Giant Triplets

"When machines and computers, profit motives and property
rights are considered more important than people, the giant
triplets of racism, materialism, and militarism are incapable of
being conquered."
Where Do We Go from Here? pp. 196-197

1

There are diseases
that kill.

They do not live
in our DNA,

they are not the result
of a crippled gene.

These toxins come
from outside us.

They exist. They make
their way in.

We sometimes act
like we don't see them.

That is one
of their symptoms.

2

Skin and color,
seeing and not

seeing. This skin
disease has roots

in the tribe. Once,
we might have

needed to fear
those who did not

look like us. Today,
it is a blindness

we cannot see.
Today, we have built

countries on this
fear. We breathe it

in from just after
birth. It takes humility

to name it and push
it away.

3

It is as simple as this:
Do you think

there is enough?
Or do you think

there is not enough?
Our answer creates

our creed. It is
as simple as this.

4

It is not just
a willingness to kill.

It is the willingness
to build a kingdom

of killing. To not
feed your children

because a faster
missile is delicious.

To not care for
your elder because

we are grateful to
a more powerful humvee.

This is what kills:
creating weapons

in every part of the
land, linking jobs

to death so no one
says no.

5

These triplets should
have been killed

at birth. But they
weren't. They were

allowed to live. Now,
they ravage

the house.

The Side of the Road

"True compassion is more than flinging a coin to a beggar;
it understands that an edifice which produces beggars needs
restructuring."
Where Do We Go from Here? p. 198

On the side of the road
sits a barely clothed woman,

wrapped in filth, breathing
in the memories of a life

that is gone. She hears
when a coin lands in her

plate. She sees the feet
of those who pass, leaving

a coin, or not leaving one.
She tries to remember

how many coins have come
today but she cannot.

She wonders if the givers
think she wants this

life, if life is what this is.
She wonders if they think

of her mother, who could
not dream of her perfect

girl squatting beside a dirt
road, hoping for one more

coin.

Time

"We are confronted with the fierce urgency of *now*. In this unfolding conundrum of life and history there is such a thing as being too late."
Where Do We Go from Here? p. 202

If only we did not live
in time,

there might always be
time

to change, to catch up,
to amend

the choices we made.

But we live in time,
which means

we can be too late,
the moment can

pass. There is a final
truth:

an eternity
during which we can

do nothing.

Chaos or Community

"We still have a choice today: nonviolent coexistence or violent coannihilation. This may well be mankind's last chance to choose between chaos and community."
Where Do We Go from Here? p. 202

1

This choice will not be
here forever.

It is here today
but like all things

it will vanish. Just
like we will.

2

Chaos is stones
coming at us

from all sides. Chaos
is the cut face,

the bleeding lips,
the broken skin,

the purple and black
wound beside the eye,

the child begging
it to stop. Chaos

is us picking up
stones and joining

the war. As soon
as I decide to harm

you, I am wounded.

3

Community is not
a world without

stones. It is a world
where we choose

never to throw them
at one another.

The Mountain Top

"… I have been to the mountain top. And I've seen the promised land. I might not get there with you but we, as a people, will get to the promised land."
—Memphis, April 3, 1968

An exhaustion rests on my skin
like sweat. Tonight I am

afire with this truth: I and we
are one. Whether I see certain

victory does not matter anymore.
Whether my children see it

is all that matters. That the children
of Memphis see it, is enough.

Tonight I am alive with this
comfort. I can let it all go.

The worst fear will eventually
come true. I will not know

its day and time until it is
here. Even then, I might not

know it. Tonight I am released
with this glory. My own eyes

have seen it. Tonight I am at peace
with this terror.

Coretta Scott King: Funeral

What do you tell your children
about their father stone still

in a casket before them?

That a bad man in Memphis
did this and so—

That our country did this
and so—

These little children
need to live

with the man who did this.
These little children need

to live with the country
that did this.

What do you tell your children?

Martin Luther King, Jr.—Epilogue

1

When his body is carried
through the streets

in a wooden wagon
older than his father.

When his children look
on his lifeless skin

with curious grief.
When his widow's face

waits in stillness, knowing
every day from now on,

can be a bullet.

2

Like the many
who killed him, he too

knew Jesus. But his life
prepared his hands for the silk

of wood. He readied his palms
for the kiss of nails.

He knew more
than knowing can say.

He bled more than blood.

3

Most days, memory
is the enemy.

But no one wants a memory.
We want

the touch. The real
man. One day

memory is all that
remains. We will all

burn down to its truth.

4

He knew memory
wedded to time

makes possible.
He knew memory

loved into the future can
crush a bullet into sand.

He knew this was not
hope or magic.

He knew memory
burned into tomorrow

is not a certainty.
Every moment waits to be used

and using time carefully
is our why.

Using time with love
is our revolution.

This is how we raise him.
This is how

we rise.

Gratitude

A book of poetry comes into the world because of the good will and hard work of many people. I am most grateful to Randall Horton and Heather Buchanan at Willow Books. They wanted these poems in the world as much as I did. Thanks also to Susannah Heschel, Peniel Joseph, and E. Ethelbert Miller for putting their words and names on this book. Thanks to Jonathan Moises Olivares for creating the beautiful cover. To Marion S. Trikosko for the taking the cover photograph. I am also grateful to Caron Martinez who first suggested a class at American University based on Dr. King's three political autobiographies. Her encouragement started my thinking about poems drawn from these same books. I owe Katy Richey a world of thanks as she was the first reader of these poems—and she is my friend. I am deep down grateful to my students in Freshman Seminar back at the University of Notre Dame, where I first taught Dr. King's work: Rosemary Caballero Francis, Judith Killen, Michelle Lichtenberger, Sean Wetjen and many more. Thanks also, to my students and colleagues at Archbishop Carroll High School and Gonzaga College High School in Washington, D.C. They have taught me a great deal about Dr. King's vision. Particular thanks go to my poetry students, Kyle Taylor, Hunter Stewart, Lucas Jung, Joseph Wete, and Jirhe Love. Thanks to Jonathan Eaker of the Library of Congress' Prints and Photographs Room. Thanks and love to Martin Espada, Lauren Marie Schmidt, Le Hinton, Dana Kinsey, Rich Villar, and Sarah Browning who teach me what it means to be a poet in America. As always, thanks to my family, chosen and born: Orlando Pinder, Jefferson Pinder, and Stevi Calandra. I'm deeply grateful to Gina, Rick, Melissa, Dave, Caitlin, Shannon, James, and Laura. Most especially to Robert.

About the Poet

Joseph Ross is the author of three books of poetry: *Ache* (2017), *Gospel of Dust* (2013) and *Meeting Bone Man* (2012). His poems appear in many places including, *The Los Angeles Times, Poet Lore, Xavier Review, The Southern Quarterly* and *Drumvoices Revue*. He has received multiple Pushcart Prize nominations and won the 2012 Pratt Library/*Little Patuxent Review* Poetry Prize. He recently served as the 23rd Poet-in-Residence for the Howard County Poetry and Literature Society in Howard County, Maryland. He teaches English and Creative Writing at Gonzaga College High School in Washington, D.C. and writes regularly at www.JosephRoss.net.

Lightning Source UK Ltd.
Milton Keynes UK
UKHW010652130920
369802UK00001B/4